From behind the plate

From behind the plate

by JOHNNY BENCH

photographed by George Kalinsky

A Rutledge Book
Prentice-Hall, Inc., Englewood Cliffs, New Jersey

ISBN: 0-13-331454-5

Text copyright © 1972 by Johnny Bench and Rutledge Books, Inc.
Photographs copyright © 1972 by George Kalinsky and Rutledge Books, Inc.

Prepared and produced by Rutledge Books, Inc.

Published by Prentice-Hall, Inc.
Englewood Cliffs, New Jersey

Library of Congress Catalog Card Number: 72-82969

Johnny Bench Enterprises, Inc.
represented by The Professionals of Cincinnati, Inc.

Printed in the United States of America

Contributor: Bill Shannon

Contents

Introduction

While attending a celebrity golf tournament in Nashville, Johnny Bench and I were invited to a party at the Governor's Mansion by Tennessee's governor Dunn. That night he was honoring the biggest names in country-and-western music, as well as a number of golf celebrities.

Johnny's biggest interest other than home runs, RBIs, catching and scoring is music. He lives and sings it. Here he would see the likes of Johnny Cash, Glen Campbell, Charley Pride, Lynn Anderson, Tennessee Ernie Ford, Bobby Goldsboro or anyone else who might appear on "Grand Ole Opry."

When we arrived at the Governor's Mansion, I found it quite fascinating to see Johnny Bench, one of baseball's biggest stars, looking around in awe as if he were a little leaguer in a room filled with Johnny Benches.

There is more to baseball than what you read about the fleet center fielder, the strapping pull hitter or the veteran right-hander on bubble gum cards. On the back of that card is a real person, a human being. That's what this book is all about.

The average fan knows very little of what a player is like off the playing field, in the dugout, in the locker room or in his personal life. How many times have we asked someone close to a celebrity, "What's he really like?"

I had the desire to do a photographic essay on one baseball player, not necessarily to get great action shots, but to give an in-depth and emotional insight to a player—to capture baseball life in an aesthetic and sensitive way with my camera.

To me, Johnny Bench was the one player in baseball who presented the most potential as a great new superstar blended with a multifaceted private life. I approached Johnny with the idea for the book and for one year, from MVP to a trying 1971 season and back to stardom in 1972, Johnny worked with me. Together we combined our efforts traveling all over the country, from his hometown, Binger, Oklahoma, to the clubhouse at Riverfront Stadium.

In helping me and my lens achieve the insight into and the atmosphere of the clubhouse, Sparky Anderson, the Reds' manager, was most gracious with his cooperation. At times, I felt that he had opened a spot on the roster for me, the way the New York Knicks' coach Red Holzman has always done for me in my role as official photographer for Madison Square Garden. Johnny Bench is MVP off the field as well as behind the plate. A special thanks to editor John Sammis who gave endlessly of his invaluable time, to Ann Smith and Jack Meyers of The Professionals of Cincinnati, Inc., and to Ellen, who makes life so beautiful.

George Kalinsky

From behind the plate

I'm a lucky guy. I'm a catcher. In any job, the more important your position, the happier you are in your work, and to my way of thinking, catching is the most important job in baseball. On a single-game basis, pitching can wield more influence on the final outcome, but in terms of individuals playing their positions effectively over the long haul, a good catcher is more valuable to his team.

There are many things required of him: he has to call the game, which means that he must be aware of possible plays, and he must take the responsibility of positioning defenses, backing up first base on ground balls to the infield and preventing men from stealing bases. And, unlike a pitcher, he must play every day.

The mental load increases when he's not hitting—and I believe a catcher is more prone to batting slumps than are other ballplayers. Most guys, unless they've just made a costly error, come back to the dugout after fielding and immediately start to think about hitting. Why didn't I get wood on the ball last time up? What pitch is working best for their pitcher and what is he likely to throw me next time up? Should I try to bunt my way on?

When I come into the dugout, my mind is working on everything but my hitting. Primarily I'm thinking catching. Unless we're in a "laugher," wherein one team has a fat lead, I'm thinking ahead to the next inning. Are their big guns due up? If they rally, what reliever will we be bringing in and what pitches will I have to concentrate on? Is our starter losing his good fastball and should I start calling for more breaking stuff?

It adds up to a busy day at the office. But I wouldn't trade it for any other job in the world. There's never a dull moment, never a time when I'm not totally involved. I've made money, many friends, seen the world, learned a lot. As I said, I'm a lucky guy.

The catcher doesn't have just the other eight men on his team to keep track of. He has a ninth man—the umpire—to consider. Though he sometimes stands on top of you, an umpire should never bother a catcher, even when he puts his hands right on you. It's something you just become accustomed to. By crouching as low as possible, I help the umpire see the pitch better. If I block him, he may miss a pitch on the corner. He won't move. He adjusts his sights to one plane. If I rise, I block him, and a pitch he can't see is a pitch he'll call a ball.

Pop-ups are murder on a catcher because the ball is traveling away from him. I've got a lot of things to watch for—objects on the field such as baseball bats left in the on-deck circle, the first baseman charging in and the dugout. I never take my eye off the ball. If the first baseman wants the ball, he's got to call me off it. If he yells, he's got the play. My prime objective is to get to the ball quickly. Then I'll have time to station myself. I'll know where the dugout is and how far I can move in any direction.

Getting the mask off shouldn't be a problem, although sometimes I get clumsy and jam a fingernail or two into my chin. If the pop-up is straight overhead, I'll hold the mask awhile until I'm sure which way the ball is going. Then I'll give it a good heave in the opposite direction.

Every umpire has his own style of calling pitches, styles which vary most widely on strikes. Eddie Vargo is direct, as loud and as good as anybody. He's a bear-down guy with enough intensity to force out the veins in his arms. Allan Gallagher, the batter, takes strike three. He's not as enthusiastic about the call as Vargo.

A ball has been hit off the plate (right) that has bounced up in the air. The reason I'm in the air also is that I'm trying to pull the ball into fair territory as fast as possible. If I'm this close to the plate, the runner hasn't gotten very far yet and I know I can get him at first. So there's no sense in letting the hit get into foul territory.

My job on a bunt is to get out on the field as fast as possible. Even before the ball reached the bat, I was springing forward. The sooner I can get to the ball, the better my chances are of turning a double play.

Because I've come out of my crouch, the umpire has no chance to see the pitch. I'm not worried about that because had the batter decided not to swing, you can bet the pitch was going outside the strike zone. I've got a problem if the batter pops the ball up behind me because I'm not going to be able to change directions readily. But that's something I can't worry about, nor can I worry about the batter's missing the pitch. My instincts are developed sufficiently by this time so that usually I can catch a pitch even if I'm out of position.

Deciding what base to throw to after fielding the ball is entirely my decision. I'm the only one of the five fielders facing the right direction. No matter who does the fielding, I call the base to which the throw goes. The decision is based on how hard the bunt was hit, who is doing the fielding and how fast the runner or runners are.

Balls that are off-mark (opposite and page 24, bottom) or balls that are going to take a short hop are balls that you have to get in front of and block with your body so that they don't get through and allow a runner to take an extra base. In Cincinnati, as in many parks, we've got synthetic turf. Generally a synthetic surface will provide a truer bounce than natural turf, which makes throws from the outfield easier to judge. But even short hops on Astroturf can give you problems, so you've got to get down and stay down.

The same holds true for wild pitches (page 24, top). The pitch bounced in front of me. I got my body in front of it, and although the ball bounced right, it bounced out in front. I got to it as fast as I could and looked to see whether the runner was going. I have picked up the ball with only one hand because it had stopped rolling. On a ball that's rolling away, I'll use the glove, almost as I would a dustpan, to scoop it into my throwing hand.

Since I'm putting on my catching gear (page 25, top), I've either been on deck when the third out was made or, more likely, I've made the third out myself. Throwing on the equipment becomes so incredibly routine I never think of it. My mind is always elsewhere.

New baseballs (page 25, bottom) are slippery, hard to grip. Before each game the umpires use a river mud, which comes in small snuff cans, to rub up game balls. But in most games, those balls are quickly used up, which means that the catcher has to rub up the new ones brought in later in the game, usually with a little homemade spit. This allows the pitcher to throw a ball with a little roughness on it so that the pitch won't get away from him.

Pitcher Ed Sprague is a man who's been around, so he might not feel that he needs advice in a tight situation. But I've got a few things on my mind. When I talk to a pitcher, it's usually either because he doesn't know the batter or because I see something that's wrong, such as a hitch in his motion. It's easy for me to spot an irregularity in a pitcher's motion but not so easy for the pitcher. I'll tell him to follow through, to get his back into the pitch, that he doesn't have to force anything. In this case, Sprague is pitching a game late in the season. I felt that he was pressing, maybe because he was anxious to remind management that he shouldn't be traded during the winter. I told him to relax, that he'd pitch better.

Manager Sparky Anderson (left) makes all the pitching changes. He's not afraid to go to the bullpen. Sometimes he comes to the mound with his mind made up. Other times he'll ask me, "What do you think?" or "Does he still have the good stuff?" I'm not going to lie to him. Nobody, not Ross Grimsley (center) or Don Gullett (above), likes to be removed from a game unless he's dead tired. Gullett's a competitor. He feels that it's his job to finish a ball game and hates to be taken out. If it's late in the season and your club's out of it, a young pitcher might be removed early. No sense taking a chance of ruining a promising arm.

Although not fast by any means, I feel that I'm a good base runner. If I'm on base, I'll check the positioning of each outfielder before a new batter comes up. Here I've scored from first on a double. I got a good jump because I knew the ball wouldn't be caught—and that's because I knew where the outfielders were stationed. Quick decisions are to some extent dependent on quick reflexes, but even without good reactions a man can become a good base runner if he works at it.

When a runner charges for home, the on-deck batter becomes the coach. After clearing the bat away from the plate area, it's his job to tell the runner whether to come in standing or to hit the dust. In this case, the on-deck batter is the pitcher (wearing a warm-up jacket). He's crouched and his hands are down, meaning "slide!" Tom Haller, the Dodgers' catcher, has to come out for the ball, which gives me plenty of plate to cross. In the photo on page 30, I'm ahead of the play and Perez is saying, "No sweat."

The catcher can't block the plate without the ball. Haller didn't get in front of me because he didn't have the ball. Blocking the plate can be accomplished many ways, including sitting in front of it, although that's not generally a healthy thing to do because you're going to get the full brunt of an angry man running as fast as he can. If you're on the plate, he's going to remove you from it with any weapon he has at his disposal—knees, shoulder or spikes.

The way I block the plate is to lay my leg in front of it, taking advantage of the fact that I'm wearing shin guards. I keep my foot toward the runner so that I don't have my knee twisted off.

Close to the ear

One of the big requisites for a catcher is a good arm. But a good arm has to be developed. It's got to be strengthened. It's got to be taken care of, and the arm muscles have to be trained to throw.

All catchers throw directly overhand. Throwing overhand keeps the ball from tailing off. Although throwing overhand won't necessarily give you the most power (a three-quarters delivery affords more speed), it gives the greatest amount of accuracy. My father taught me when I was very young to throw only overhand, so it comes naturally to me now.

I strengthen my arm by throwing hard and for distance. The distance between home and second base is 127 feet 3 inches, so I work up to where I'll be throwing in practice as far as 200 feet. This is using the same principle that batters apply when they swing a leaded bat to make the real one seem lighter.

For me, then, working on my throwing is as important as batting practice—except when I'm in a hitting slump.

I try to get the big part of the seams of the baseball across my fingertips. This gives me a better grip, and the rotation on the ball comes up and over in a straight line to the base, helping to keep the ball on line. In practice or when throwing for keeps, I bring my arm forward as close to my ear as possible. The closer to my ear I keep my arm, the more overhand I'll be able to throw the ball.

When I'm trying to throw out a runner, I'll aim directly at the pitcher's chest, provided that he's on a direct line from me to second base. Some pitchers fall off the mound, in which case I'll aim directly over the pitching rubber. But most pitchers hang around in front of the mound after delivery, usually to be in position to field a ball hit up the middle. If I'm throwing to second, their job is to get out of the way because I'm not going to change the line of my throw. I've come very close to hitting pitchers, but I prefer to have them there because they give me a good target. If I'm on target (pitcher's chest), I know that my throw has enough behind it to reach the base.

Some wrist popping

Hitting—and I should know—is a difficult thing to do well. I'm a power hitter, so what I have to say about the art may or may not apply to all hitters. However, in general, the essentials are applicable to all.

Hitting is a lot of essentials, most of which have to be done right if a ballplayer is going to hit well. Hitting means knowing the pitcher and being aware of the situation—the number of men on base, the score, the inning and the pitcher's best pitch. Hitting means taking the right stride, making contact, getting the hands moving, keeping the eyes on the ball, opening the hips, driving the shoulder and transferring weight. If you do all these things correctly and your reflexes and eyes are good enough, you'll probably get a hit 3 out of 10 times at bat.

Loosening up (right) is often more important for a catcher than a hitter. I sweat a lot behind the plate, and when I come back to the dugout to sit, my muscles tighten up. Since the pitchers aren't going to let me loosen up in the box, I do as much as I can in the on-deck circle. I use my own bat, as well as a model with added weight in the form of a leaded sleeve. The wood bat feels lighter when I'm actually hitting. I get the feeling that I can really pop those wrists.

Long-ball hitters like myself generate the most power by swinging from the end of the bat and going out after the pitch. I throw a lot of weight into the pitch and I'm always aggressive. Having strong arms as well as wrists is a factor in drilling the ball, but nothing helps if your timing isn't right.

Before swinging, my weight is more on my right leg than my left, but during the swing, and especially afterward, the weight is transferred to my left side. Although my left leg is bent (right), the position is still called "hitting off a stiff left side." All my weight is being absorbed by my left thigh. The muscles in there are as taut as possible. I'm getting power in the area from the tops of my thighs to the belt buckle.

Not only is quickness in the wrists important but the roll of the wrists is often crucial when trying to drive the ball out. I try to keep the knuckles as lined up as possible so that when I swing, I can't help rolling the wrists. In effect, a good wrist roll spins the bat so that the ball jumps off it.

My father always told me to keep my eye on the ball and let the other things hang in there. Some hitters, such as Pete Rose, will follow the ball all the way into the catcher's glove. For me, that's just not possible, but it is important for me to watch the ball for as long as I can. Hitting a baseball is a lot like hitting a golf ball. You've got to pivot. A pivot transfers the weight properly, but then you can't let the bat fly through unless you open the hips. Without a pivot, you can't power the ball. The hips get around, the shoulder drives through and the hands and wrists are right behind. Last, the bat crosses the plate, hopefully with your full weight behind it. My problem is that I swing at bad pitches. I guess I'm just too anxious to smash the ball.

This is a good stride—long but not so long that it will throw your timing off. The hips have already begun their move. On the right is a situation presented to all power hitters. The pitch is up and in, termed a "brushback," "knockdown" or "purpose pitch." Under my breath, it's called other things. It's the way a pitcher lets you know he's boss, that he's not about to let you take any plate away from him.

Slump. That's what this picture is all about. I don't bunt for a hit unless I'm not hitting. When you're slumping, you sometimes resort to means other than swinging the bat to get on base. Even with my slower speed, I can get on with a good bunt because the infield is playing back so far. With a man on third, I'll never squeeze because I feel that with my power I should at least get the ball into the outfield far enough to score the runner. Here I may have bunted at a pitch just below the strike zone, but once you've decided to bunt for a hit, you're pretty well committed. And if you don't go after it, you've lost the element of surprise.

On the periphery

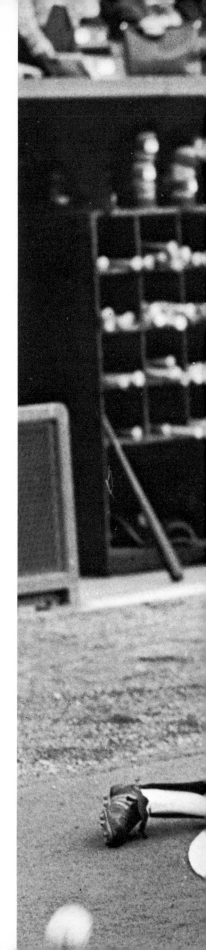

A ballplayer spends a lot more time at his job than the time it takes to play a game. Depending on his manager's time schedule, he arrives at the park anywhere from three to four hours before a game. On the field there's constant activity—batting practice, fielding practice, fly shagging, wind sprints for pitchers and autograph signing. After the game he talks to reporters, grabs a bite to eat, showers and signs more autographs. Every three or four days he's running to catch a plane after which he can spend as many as five hours in the air and another hour traveling to another hotel.

Before a game, if you have no specific assignment, you find things to keep you busy, to keep the muscles loose. There are a hundred variations on the game of pepper. How many cute girls are watching sometimes determines the amount of horseplay (right). If you're in a tight pennant race, high jinks keep you relaxed. If you're way ahead, they pass the time. If you're hopelessly out of things, the clowning—and there's less of it—is confined to the clubhouse. All you think about then is getting the damn season over and starting again the following spring.

Signing autographs on the field is a hassle, pure and simple. While your team has the field, you've got a number of things to do, as I've mentioned. You've got only so much time and most of it is taken. When you leave the field, you've got about 40 minutes until game time. You want to take advantage of those 40 minutes, so any signing you do comes off that time. What I try to do is if I see a quiet group of three or four people, I come over and sign, then break away quickly. But quiet, small groups are rare. Usually everybody's leaning over the rail, screaming, screaming, screaming. If you don't sign every card, they think you're a bum. But you can't please everybody, there's just no way. After the game is the ideal time to get autographs, when I've got a few leisurely moments and I'm more relaxed.

Like many dugouts in the new stadiums, Cincinnati's is more walk-in than step-down, with a platform in front adjacent to the artificial turf. Just before the home team is called to the field, most players on the team mill around in front of the dugout since they'll be sitting for the next couple of hours. Coach Ted Kluszewski watches the field; I check out a female fan. I've hardly ever gotten a date by spotting a girl in the stands, going over to her and starting a conversation. I tried that once but was mobbed by other fans. I can't even talk to my folks if they're at a game. Everything has to wait until afterward.

In the clubhouse

Baseball is fun to play because of the guys who play it. You build a great camaraderie, much of which is cemented in the privacy of the clubhouse. Generally speaking, the home team's clubhouse is the nicer of the two, although in the new parks, that's changing. In Cincinnati, we have a great clubhouse—carpeted, spacious and clean.

No holds are barred in the clubhouse. If you have a problem, physical or mental, you discuss it with your teammates. Everybody seems to know everybody else's hang-ups. There's a great trust between players. In Cincinnati, we're a group of 25. There are no cliques.

It's no difficult thing for ballplayers to like one another. You're all athletes, and to that extent you all have common goals. Your likes and dislikes are about the same. You make eternal friends playing baseball. Sure, after 170 days with the same faces, they begin looking a little ugly, but by the time spring training rolls around, everybody there is looking for everybody else and we're happy to see each other.

At the right, the game is over and it's time to go in. I've got two or three gloves because I might have had to play first base or the outfield.

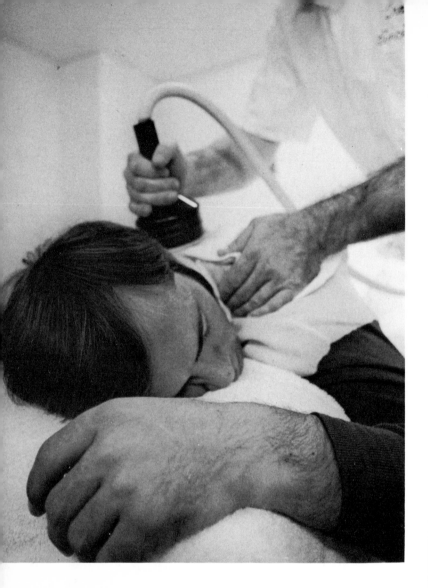

Our trainer is Bill Cooper, a guy we call "Doc," although the only professional aspect of his life other than that of trainer is that he raises poodles. Although I'm young enough so that I rarely have need to see the trainer, in the eighth grade I did hurt my back. I've had some sacroiliac problems ever since, which is what Doc is working on (right). After a long weekend of baseball and sundry other activities, my body's hurting. A luxury rub (above) hits the spot. A good way to relieve tension and relax is the use of a vibrator.

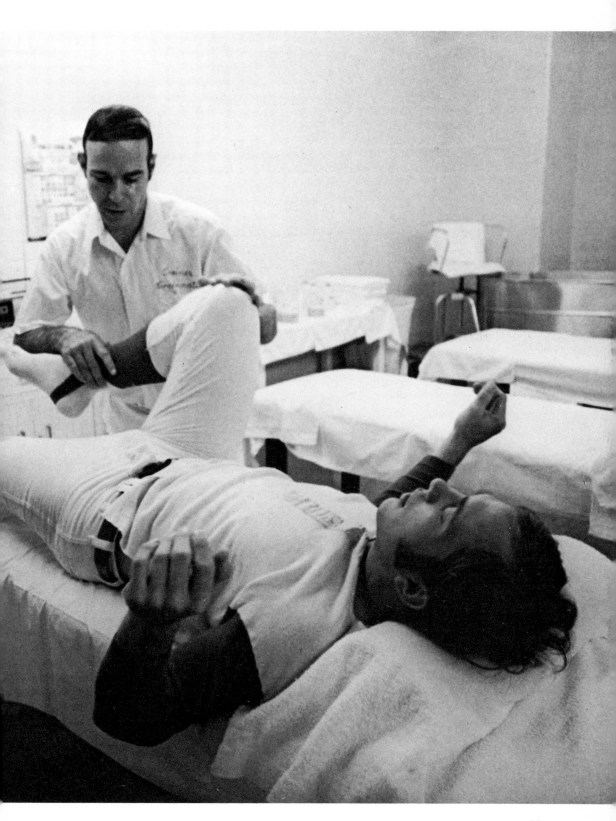

An injury to a key player can absolutely ruin a club's pennant chances, as the Reds demonstrated in 1971. Bobby Tolan tore an Achilles tendon prior to the season and the Big Red Machine plummeted from first place.

Bobby worked religiously on a special weight machine to build back his scarred leg. Although some of the guys on the club secretly wrote him off, Bobby's determination never slacked and he returned in 1972, running the opposition to distraction.

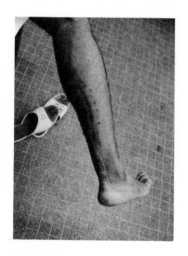

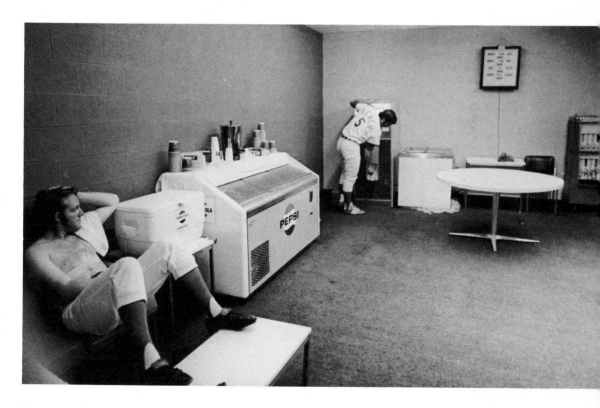

Both pictures here were taken during the 40-minute break between batting practice and game time. Jim McGlothlin cools it on the bench following a series of wind sprints. Pitchers sprint every day (except when pitching) to keep their legs in shape to go nine innings every four days. I'm over at the popcorn machine, courtesy Tommy Helms. Helms loves popcorn so much that he got somebody to buy the team a popcorn machine and had it shipped to the clubhouse. There's been talk of removing the food and soda dispensers so that we can concentrate more on baseball.

Keeping your mind on baseball at all times can be a problem. That carpet makes a nice practice surface for sharpening up your golf game.

Hal McCrae (right) is the Reds' Flip Wilson, resident pantomime expert. Here he does his routine of the lost pop fly. In a quieter moment (below) before a game, Bobby Tolan listens to his cassette machine, an item that a lot of players carry around now. Ten to one he's thinking about the ankle.

Tommy Tucker (Helms) and Bull (Al Ferrara) if not at the ball park are at the racetrack. They think up more idiot's delights than you could dream of, including (left) the horseplayer's handshake. Below, Willie Smith tells Lee May, both first basemen, the correct way to come off the bag. We call Lee "the Mechanical Man" or "Robot." Some machine. All three of these guys now have been traded. It's something we learn to live with, but you can't help missing them.

Saturday afternoon before a baseball game means a football game. Photo by Tommy Helms.

Only two or three of us on the club aren't married, which presents a problem —we get most of the mail from girls. Naturally, if you're a star, like Pete Rose, you'll get hundreds of letters every day. But if you're a bachelor, you get an additional load. A lot of letters are requests for pictures, which we sign and send (bottom). Most requests (balls are the most popular) are taken care of by my secretary, whom I hired to do just that. I read each letter, which is great since just about 99 percent of them are complimentary. A few berate— "How come you did this?" or "Why can't you do that?" but most are nice. I get letters from girls who want to meet me through a mutual friend, or so they say, but most of these are from the younger ones. The Giants asked me to sign the huge ball (top) for one of the fans. I wish some of the fastballs in this league looked that big.

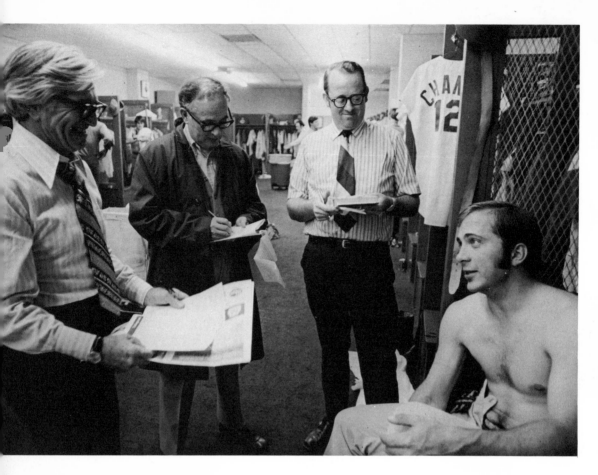

If you have a good night, the writers come around. Whether they're Dick Young from New York, Earl Lawson from Cincinnati or Jim Ferguson from Dayton, they all want the same thing—some kind of inside story. I give them all the same answer or I'd go crazy. The writers treat us well. We reciprocate. Occasionally we'll build up pretty good friendships, although not like it used to be when everyone traveled together by train. Dick and I joke (above). He commented on Cincinnati: "I used to know a lot of good-looking girls here."

"Yeah," I said, "Babe Ruth used to date them."

Before a night game I'll eat at 3:30 or 4:00, so I'm a little hungry when the game's over. There's always food around, and a rotating menu keeps you interested in anything from lasagna to fried chicken. Sometimes, when you lose, you're not hungry—you just want to go home.

ittle John and Big Klu clean up a___ a game. Can you believe the size of that man?

Believe it or not, *Cosmopolitan* was interested in me before they latched on to Burt Reynolds. Here, *Cosmo's* Body of the Year gladly heads for the relaxation of a nice hot shower.

Going home

Oklahoma isn't all flat. West of Oklahoma City, the geography is what you'd call "rolling farmland." East of Sayre, about two-and-a-half miles past Resume Speed, in a little valley, lies Binger—my hometown.

The soil there is sandy loam, just right for peanuts, cotton, wheat, maize and alfalfa. Mostly peanuts, though. Binger, Oklahoma, the Peanut Capital of the World! Population 600 at the height of the tourist season. I knew everybody who lived there. I can't imagine growing up anywhere else.

I lived with real salt-of-the-earth people, people who weren't trying to kill themselves getting things done, people who had less so they appreciated more. There was no rush to grow up, no pressure to get out and "do" something. Childhood seemed longer.

I like city life better, now. It's faster paced with more action, more travel, more to do. I've been given more than a taste of it and I've come to thrive on it. But Binger gave me a sense of peace and a base from which to evaluate all else. When I get out of baseball, I want to settle in a small town. I want my kids to grow up slowly.

The last three pictures are all of the place where I lived—not the Beverly Hills Hotel, but home. I was born in Oklahoma City, December 7, 1947, but we soon moved on out, settling in and picking up from Oklahoma's glory towns—Kiner Creek, Aaron Falls, Lindsay. In Lindsay, Dad took on a liquefied petroleum company and distributed gas to neighboring towns. Most of his customers came from the Binger area, so we moved our truck and petroleum tanks to Binger.

That was when I was four. Two years later we added an extension to our house (page 86, lower part of house) to make two more bedrooms. On page 85, at the right of the house, you can see the tanks for which we supplied fuel. The fuel was for heating homes and for cooking. We were one of the few families not heavily into farming.

That's not to say I didn't farm. Ever since I can remember, I was picking cotton or peanuts. School started August 1, let out the beginning of September so that the kids could help with the peanut harvest and then opened again in November.

At the right is our neighbor's backyard, fenced in now. We used to store Dad's equipment in the shed or leave it out lying around. Just as long as it stayed off the basketball court. That basket's not much different now—we wore it out pretty good. I guess I liked basketball as much as I liked anything.

We really never got much out of cattle, although occasionally we'd try to rope a few. They mostly roamed around, fattening up, until someone took them to market.

Billy Rosser's gas station, the town's big business, is also the town's second main gathering place, next to the pool hall. The old guys sit around at night, away from home, and shoot the breeze. Del Carey, in the hat, along with Hugh Haley, took me everywhere as a kid—ball games, events, speeches—and never let me pay a cent. Well, maybe I didn't exactly offer.

We used to sit in a row at ball games, me on the outside. Change, passed from hand to hand, ended in my fist. Sure, they got their hot dogs and beer but never the leftover money. Del's asking me where it is. By the pickup truck, Binger's most common conveyance, is Jess Lynn, attired in Binger's most common dress. The truck is splattered with mud and tobacco juice.

The only stop signs in seven-block-long Binger.

We've got a lot of Binger signs to remind us where we are. The blacksmith shop sort of died when Dodge Freeman did, but the lumber company's still going. That's been there for as long as I can remember. The gas station sells my T-shirts.

I never had much to do with town hall meetings, but for 10 years I had perfect attendance at church, more than I can say for myself now. I'm a Southern Baptist. I believe in the Hereafter; I believe in God. He's the main Man.

JOHNNY BENCH
President 4
Basketball 1, 2, 3, 4
   Caddo County All Star
   State Tourn. All Star
   All State Team
   Prep All America
Baseball 1, 2, 3, 4
   All State
Honor Roll 1, 2, 3, 4
Senior Play
Annual Staff
Valedictorian

SHARON SCOTT
Vice President 4
Glee Club 1, 2, 3, 4
Vocal Trio 1, 3, 4
FFA Sweetheart 2
FHA 1, 2, 3, 4
FHA Secretary 4
Senior Play
Annual Staff
Salutatorian

ANN DAVIS
Secretary 4
Basketball 1, 2, 3, 4
Softball 1, 2, 3
Cheerleader 4
FHA 1, 2, 3, 4
FHA Secretary 4
Class Queen 1
Senior Play
Annual Staff

I graduated in a class of 21 students. They're all married and most of them are living other places, doing their own things. Their folks are still here, though. They gave me a twenty-fourth birthday party. The whole town turned out for the celebration in the auditorium. I still can't believe they did that.

A lot's changed down at the field. We never had a roof nor bleachers nor even a fence in the outfield. We had to leg out the home runs, which weren't too frequent because the wind used to blow from off the farm-land and come right in over center field. There's an old dam about 400 feet out toward left center. I hit it once. Must have been windless that day.

JOHNNY BENC

The Giants:
a set in
Cincinnati

For a single man, there's really not much difference between playing at home or away. For a married ballplayer, it's a different story. He's got to leave a wife and kids when he hits the road. He's always concerned that everything's going to be all right, that nobody's going to get sick, that the house won't be burglarized or whatever, because he's not there to help out.

Playing at home is convenient for me—I can take care of business and visit my family, and I know where to go to relax after a game. But home is where the pressure comes from. When I slumped in 1971, the fans let me know it. I was booed for the first time in my life. I was hurt and upset, probably to a greater degree than anyone knew.

I tried too hard to do not only a good job but a better job than either the fans or myself had a right to expect. Now that it's happened once, maybe I'll be able to accept it the next time, be able to understand it and not let it bother me. Maybe.

Before each game I like to sing the national anthem. But not when Stan Landes is so close. I don't think Stan appreciates a quality baritone.

After more than 20 years in professional baseball, the enthusiasm that Willie Mays brings into a ball park is as strong as ever. Although he's lost a little of his old skill, his pride and enthusiasm and natural strength still carry him. I know he wants to play ball as long as he can, but as he said, "I'll play as long as I feel I can honestly help my team. When it gets to the point where I embarrass either the team or myself, I'll quit."

Willie's still fast, still quick. I read in *Sports Illustrated*
that a man 85 years old is still able to react with 85-per-
cent effectiveness. If Willie's playing ball when he's 85,
I won't be surprised. At the right he's loosening up while
talking with Alex Grammas in the dugout.

Only a few times in history has a catcher tagged two men out at home on the same play. I wasn't destined to be one of them.

The Giants had two runners on, Tito Fuentes at first, Ken Henderson at second. Bobby Bonds, at bat, had driven the ball deep to right center, well past Pete Rose. Fuentes realized that the ball wasn't going to be caught, but Henderson wasn't sure. Besides, he was in no hurry. If the ball was caught, he would tag and go on to third. If it got through, he had plenty of time to score. By the time he realized that it was safe to run, Fuentes had caught up to him.

I saw both runners, knew where both were and knew I had time to get both of them. The throws from Rose to Helms to me were perfect, the last a one-bouncer that I could gauge easily because of the consistency of Astroturf.

And then, unbelievably, the ball hit a small separation in the Astroturf where the synthetic meets dirt, just in front of the plate. The ball jumped and bounced over my head. Both runners were safe.

In the second game I hit a home run to win it for us. Two games down, one to go, although it wasn't quite as simple as that. Tempers fly in a pennant race (right). Fuentes hit a long flyball with Henderson on first. Ken, making up for his previous lack of nerve, flew across second and was churning for third when the ball was caught. He returned to first in time but failed to touch second base on his way back. We threw to second and Henderson was called out. A tremendous argument ensued, made more vocal by Giant fielders who came out because the play had ended the inning.

You see a lot of arguments like this after plays at the plate, but they are always about a tag or interference call, never over balls and strikes. A manager is not allowed to argue a called pitch. That's left to the catcher. If a good pitch is called a ball, I'll usually speak up: "Now *that's* a good pitch" or "Where was it?" Sometimes I'll really get frustrated and lay it on the umpire. I might get in trouble, but I might just get everybody to bear down a little harder.

We really wanted to win that third game to salvage something of a bad season. A large crowd turned out, so we felt we owed something to their loyalty. But Juan Marichal, who throws nine kinds of pitches at 20 different speeds, came back to beat us. The best I could do was a long-fly out with Perez in scoring position.

Bachelorhood: the

good life

One of the things I've been lucky enough to afford is a nice place to live. I bought a multilevel condominium in Cincinnati overlooking the river. It's not Wilt Chamberlain's place, but it'll do.

At the right is Cincinnati's Don McLean. Buck Owens sent me the guitar. I'd love to be able to play, but I'm not a natural, have never taken lessons and have wide fingers that insist on covering two strings at once.

I have never had any musical instruction. I remember I used to laugh at a kid in Binger who took piano lessons because I thought it was a sissy thing to do. I wish I'd been the one who was the sissy.

Dianne, a stewardess from Washington, drops by when she's in Cincinnati. And I do play chess.

Dianne and I check out the icebox for something fit to eat. Usually there's not much around. Since I'm out of town so often, the food in the refrigerator generally leaves something to be desired when I return. Eggs hold up pretty well, though.

In the kitchen, business associates Ann Smith and Jack Meyers hash over a contract of some kind.

No pad is complete without tape deck and stereo. Whether country and western, acid rock or middle-of-the-road, music is a super friend of mine.

I don't smoke and hardly ever drink. I guess music's my thing. A perfect evening would be dinner out and then back to the pad with a pretty girl, a few friends and good sounds.

A few years ago Pete Rose and I went into the car business. We called it, imaginatively, Rose and Bench Lincoln-Mercury. Although it no longer exists, I managed to buy a Lincoln Continental from the business. It's fully air-conditioned, fully everything-ed in fact. I've got to admit it's a nice way to live. It's comfortable and, like all nice things, I enjoy it.

A view from the top.

The first-floor study serves as both trophy room and office. I'm President of Johnny Bench Enterprises, Inc., and a stockholder in The Professionals of Cincinnati, Inc., capably run by Jack Meyers and Ann Smith from our downtown Carew Tower office. The Professionals, Inc., represent me in all of my nonplaying activities. The outside money I make is as important as the money I earn from playing baseball. I came along the first year of the free-agent draft, 1965, and was further affected by a rule which prohibited progressive bonuses. I signed for $14,000 and the maximum first-year salary—$500 a month.

Johnny Bench Enterprises, Inc., handles other athletes, tries to land commercials and other endorsements and invests in land and other long-term ventures. The number of outside activities a ballplayer can get involved in is limited because of the amount of time he has to devote to actually playing baseball. I'm trying to set up some kind of a future so that when I retire, I'll have a job and an income.

130

I like the way I live. I hope it can continue. You have to be able to live your life your way. If you can be honest with yourself, not hurt anybody and make yourself happy, you've got it made. Once you start doing things you don't really care about doing, you soon find out you're not a very happy person inside. When a person is happy with himself and his life, his happiness becomes infectious—it spreads to those around him. A little more happiness, a little less hate and the world could be a heck of a lot nicer place.

A birthday for dad

In 1971, I threw a surprise birthday party for Dad. Nothing could have made me happier. My parents have given me everything—a sense of morality, a family life, a desire to do well. It tickles me to death to know that I'm now in a position to do something for my parents.

Dad loves golf and I've been able to buy him a new set of clubs. I've been able to supply him new clothes, a car, time to relax. When I came to Cincinnati, I urged the family to join me. Dad was reluctant at first, but he loved baseball so much I guess he couldn't pass up the chance to play it vicariously through his son. He made a deal to run a motel in Cincinnati and made the move. Mom and Sis live there with Dad. Mom runs the place. Dad plays golf.

The party was a success. Dad was surprised (right). He had expected only a card game.

The family (left) poses with Dad's cake before demolishing it. To my left are Mom, Dad, sister Marilyn and brother William. But even at a birthday party, there's business to attend to (above). Sometimes the demands get to be too much, but if I don't do it now, I may never get another chance.

On camera

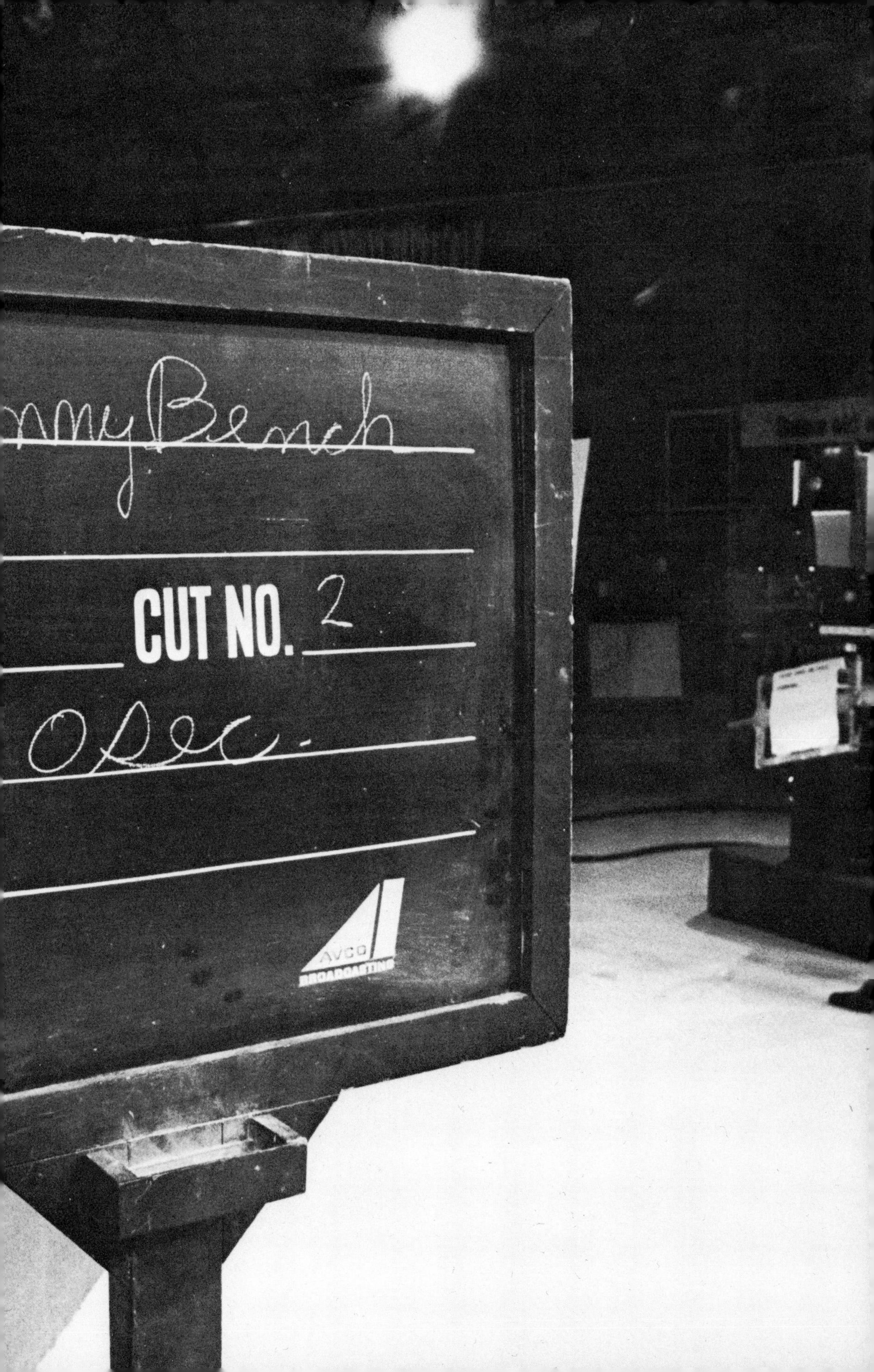
CUT NO. 2
AVCO
BROADCASTING

Early in 1971, Stadium Productions, Inc., of New York, a company that had handled the Willis Reed show and had worked with Joe Namath, came to me proposing that I do a television show for 23 weeks. It was to be a talk-show format and was to be called "MVP." Sounded like fun.

It was, until the moment I had to face the camera. My first guests were Bob Hope and Willie Mays. I was given just a general outline of what to do. When the director pointed "you're on" to me, I sort of went into a stupor. Bob and Willie took over, carrying the show, but it was all downhill from there on. We never made a pilot nor did we have to retape a single show the whole year.

It was a great experience—still is, since the show was renewed. It taught me to relax, and I met a lot of great people, some of whom have become lifelong friends. A singer, for instance, has a lot in common with a ballplayer. We're both professional performers. I like music; he generally likes sports. When we get together, it's a mutual-admiration-society thing—and great times.

After the show, I talk here with Glen Campbell and Jim Lefevbre. Jim, with Wes Parker of the Dodgers, has formed a group called Athletes for Youth, an anti-drug-oriented group. The three of us taped a show about drugs. Naturally, I'm also dead against them. I feel that when a kid goes to college, he should decide then and there what he wants to do. With a goal and direction, he will stay away from depending on drugs. I get involved with the drug problem, and though it sounds clichéd, I want to save just one kid from turning to drugs.

After each show is a question-and-answer session (right, top). Before that, you never know. We held a surprise party in Cincinnati for David Hartman (right, bottom). I gave him an autographed bat. On the show, he presented me with a Hartman autographed model.

A game
of golf

Two years ago I played in the American Airlines golf tournament and the Bob Hope Desert Classic as an amateur teamed with a pro. I met a lot of people involved with golf, including a group representing the Country and Western Association out of Nashville. They asked me to compete in their tournament the following year, right after the season ended.

When 1971 ended, I wanted to get away. Luckily I hadn't many commitments—I wasn't going to be too popular on the banquet circuit. I decided to travel to Tampa, where the instructional circuit was in full swing and where I could work on my batting while my muscles were still loose from the season. I took the long route, stopping in Nashville for the Country and Western tournament.

My partner was Bruce Devlin (putting, right). We had a ball. Finished third.

The tournament went beautifully, even though the weather soured. Even Tennessee's governor, the Honorable Winfield Dunn (far left), came out to play.

I first met Lee Trevino (above) in a tournament in Montreal. He remembered me and brought Tennessee Ernie Ford into the locker room for introductions. They're a beautiful pair, each as crazy as the other. Lee was staying at Bobby Goldsboro's house in Nashville, where we all went one night and told stories until the sun came up.

It's nice they know who you are.

Not my best swing. Devlin's nonplussed.

The golf tournament was highlighted by a party at the Governor's Mansion. A ton of country-and-western singers were on hand, including Johnny Cash, as well as all the golfers and hangers-on like myself. I brought a date, Sue Conlan, but occasionally found time to talk with the hostesses. Bobby Goldsboro (far right) chaperones while waiting to sing. He broke his hand in a cycling accident.

Lee Trevino and his wife make me feel at home. At one point we switched name tags. Lee got mine. While he was wearing it, a lady came up to him, said it was a pleasure to meet him and asked him whether anyone had ever told him he looked a lot like Lee Trevino? "Yeah," he answered, "and it just bugs the hell out of me."

Just like an old Oklahoma country-party barbecue.

The Mets: a set on the road

As I said, sometimes I'm more comfortable on the road than at home. I don't get booed on the road. If I'm in a slump, I can slip away to a movie or sit isolated in my hotel room. And there's always the team around to lift the spirits.

Most ball parks today are so standardized that there's little home-field advantage. Shea Stadium and Riverfront Stadium are both symmetrical. Caroms play the same; the distances are equivalent. Riverfront has Astroturf, but the Mets don't tailor their field to their team, anyway. It used to be that you could adjust your field to the type of team you had. Now you more or less have to adjust your team.

New York's not my favorite place to play. Home runs don't come as easily as they do in some other parks, such as Atlanta and Philly. And the kids—they know more about baseball than I ever dreamed about. I sign a kid's baseball in front of the Biltmore Hotel on my way to the game, and when I get to the park, the same kid is waiting for me with a program in one hand, a pen in the other. I don't know how he got there or what he's going to do with the autographs, but that's New York.

Coming into the series you see pictured on these pages, the Mets led their division by three-and-a-half games while we trailed the Dodgers by a half-game. Both teams were up. It promised to be interesting.

Pregame practice for me consists mostly of shagging long flyballs. The home team has the field for practice first, so while the Mets were working out, we held a meeting, which we do at the start of every series.

The purpose of these meetings is to run over the other team's lineup. We'll listen to up-to-the-minute scouting reports—what batters are going good, who's having trouble handling the curve, who's not swinging at certain pitches.

What the current reports don't tell me I'll know from past experience, but even that knowledge sometimes is useless since pitchers are rarely consistent from one game to the next. Even though Gary Nolan may have gotten Cleon Jones on an outside slider the last time they faced each other in a crucial situation, I can't call for the same pitch the next time if Gary isn't throwing his slider the same way.

Generally, I won't worry too much about whether to call for my pitcher's best pitch or to call for a pitch to the batter's weakness. The overriding factor in any tight situation is to keep the pitch down. Low balls have a tendency to stay in the park.

Some pitchers are fast enough to throw the ball by the hitter when they have to. When Tom Seaver, for instance, gets in a jam, chances are he'll rear back and throw the fast one. Even if the batter's set for the pitch, he probably won't get the bat around in time. The best hitter in the world is only going to hit between 3 and 4 times out of 10.

A lead-off man's goal is to get on base. Bud Harrelson starts off for the Mets. He's a .230 hitter, but he's fast and draws a lot of walks. Our prime objective with him is to throw strikes. We try to do that with the lead-off hitter in each inning. It's vital to start an inning with an out.

Our next objective is to get ahead of each batter. Once you get that first strike, you're in a better position to outguess the batter. When you're behind on the count, you've got to come to him. He can set himself for a certain pitch because he's got a strike to waste.

With runners on base, pitching philosophy doesn't change. We don't throw more fastballs as a protection against the steal because generally a pitcher throws more fastballs than breaking stuff anyway. When a runner reaches third, it's doubly important to keep the pitches down to prevent a sacrifice fly. How carefully you work with the bases loaded depends to some extent on who the on-deck hitter is. In other words, would you rather give the guy who is up a good pitch to hit or do you take a chance on a walk because the due hitter isn't as dangerous?

Actually, it's much simpler than all that. Just keep everybody off base and you're in.

In the first game, nobody scored until the fourth when Bobby Tolan singled, went to second on a throwing error and I managed to send a good outside slider into the left-field bullpen (above).

Our report on John Milner was that he likes high fastballs. Who doesn't? Like true believers we threw Milner a high fastball, which he smashed off the scoreboard to cut our lead to a run (above right).

The game tightened. Although an off-year for Pete Rose, the Mets respected him enough to keep him honest.

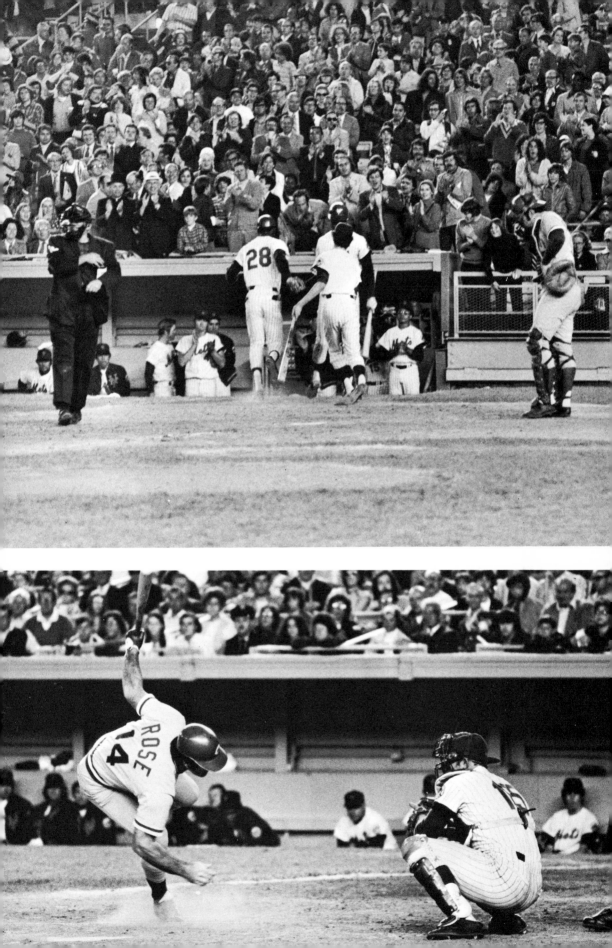

Rusty Staub likes to wait for the fastball he can hit out. In the sixth, with Agee on first, we dutifully kept the ball down to Staub and he grounded into a double play, Concepcion to Morgan to Perez (photos).

But we worked too carefully to the next hitter, Milner, and walked him. When Cleon Jones doubled, John turned on the wheels and scored from first to tie the game.

Agee singled home the winner in the seventh. We lost the first leg, and while the Mets held their position, we fell a game and a half behind the Dodgers.

Card games flourish on the road. Away from home, sometimes with little to do, some of the guys will go out to
the park early, get half-dressed, then sit for an hour or
two at the card table and insult each other. Additional
pregame rituals: batting practice and a seminar with
Yogi Berra.

We were up for game two. Dropping a game in the standings produced a little more adrenaline. We had a sort of do-or-die attitude, even though the season wasn't half over.

We jumped on Gary Gentry in the first inning. After Rose struck out, Joe Morgan walked, Tolan singled, I walked and Tony Perez (right) brought us all home with a double to left.

In the sixth Joe Hague (above) gave us the winner with a home run as we won, 6–3. The Dodgers lost, so after two games we were back where we started—but we felt the momentum building.

New York's lead was cut to two-and-a-half games, so they retaliated with Willie Mays, who went two for three and scored one of their two runs. But we scored four in the first, defensed well and left the field tied with the Dodgers.

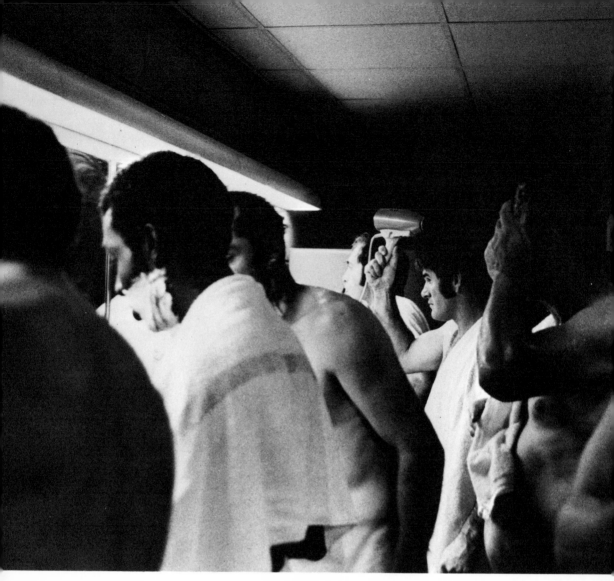

After the game we crowd into the beauty parlor. Check out Pete Rose, "the Last of the Crew Cuts." The fashion scene is a whole new thing with today's ballplayers.

We travel everywhere by charter jet. There's no waiting, no airport hassle, no pressures. I really can't say that the travel bothers me at all. Good-bye, George.

You grow up with a dream. You want to be a baseball player. You hold the people who play baseball in very high esteem.

Then you make it. You're a baseball player. You find out how human people can be. We all make mistakes, not only Johnny Bench, but all athletes. If we can get these mistakes down to a small number, we succeed.

To do that, you've got to give 100 percent. You've got to get involved, pursue with desire—then you can conquer anything . . . baseball, politics, business, the arts. Whatever you decide to be, try to be the best. Second place is coming in high, but it's not bad to try to be number one. At least I hope it's not, because that's what I want.